Volcano

IMAGES OF HAWAI'I'S VOLCANOES

Photography by

Douglas Peebles

Mutual Publishing

All images of Kīlauea Volcano were taken in Hawai'i
Volcanoes National Park unless noted otherwise.

Library of Congress Catalog Card Number: 2003107831

ISBN-10: 1-56647-603-8
ISBN-13: 978-1-56647-603-4

First Printing, November 2003
Second Printing, April 2004
Third Printing, June 2005
Fourth Printing, September 2006
Fifth Printing, February 2008

Mutual Publishing, LLC
1215 Center Street, Suite 210
Honolulu, Hawai'i 96816
Ph: (808) 732-1709 Fax: (808) 734-4094
e-mail: info@mutualpublishing.com
www.mutualpublishing.com
Printed in Taiwan.

Rivers of lava flowing along the slopes of Puʻu ʻŌʻō Vent.

A volcanic fireworks display. Kīlauea Volcano

Kīlauea Volcano

The sunset sky is accentuated by the orange glow of molten lava. Kīlauea Volcano

Voluminous clouds of steam from the meeting of lava and water. Kīlauea Volcano

A thin river of molten yellow lava reaches the sea. Kīlauea Volcano

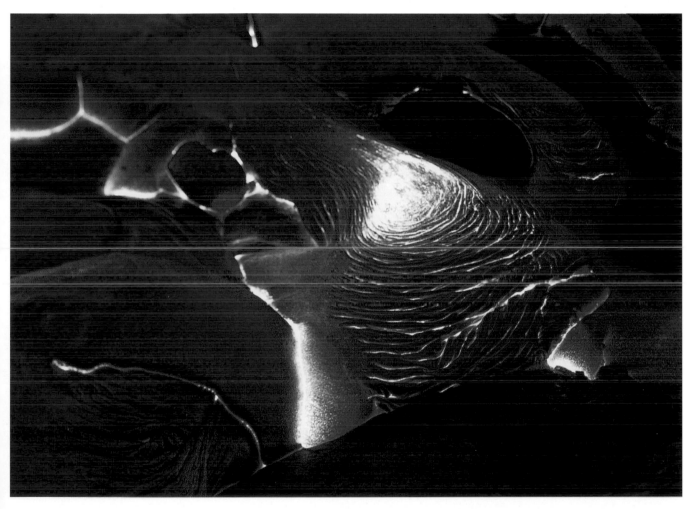

A slowly cooling pond of pāhoehoe lava. Kīlauea Volcano

The native 'ama'u fern grows quickly on new lava flows. Kīlauea Iki

Ceremonial dancers bring hoʻokupu (gifts) to Ka Hoʻolaʻa Ana Investiture. Kīlauea Caldera

Puʻu ʻŌʻō Vent, Kīlauea Volcano.

Molten lava oozes from beneath a crust of hardend rock. Kīlauea Volcano

Veinlike cracks in hardened crust reveal molten lava beneath. Kīlauea Volcano

A sky light provides a glimpse of lava flowing beneath the crust of this lava tube.

Clouds of steam and smoke billow from the ocean touched by lava. Kīlauea Volcano

New plant life grows in the volcanic landscape. Kīlauea Iki

Homes set ablaze by lava flowing through Kalapana.

Asphalt burns under the slow approach of the lava. Kīlauea Volcano

A narrow river of lava follows the path of older flows.
Kīlauea Volcano

A bubbling lava lake pours from an open-sided cone.
Kīlauea Volcano

A thin crust has formed on the surface of this active lava lake within Pu'u 'Ō'ō cone.

A lunar-like landscape of cinder cones on Hualālai Volcano.

Steam rising above the cliffs overlooking a lake of lava.
Puʻu ʻŌʻō Vent, Kīlauea Volcano

A fountain of lava violently explodes into the sky.
Kīlauea Volcano

Small fountains play along the edges of this lava lake. Puʻu ʻŌʻō

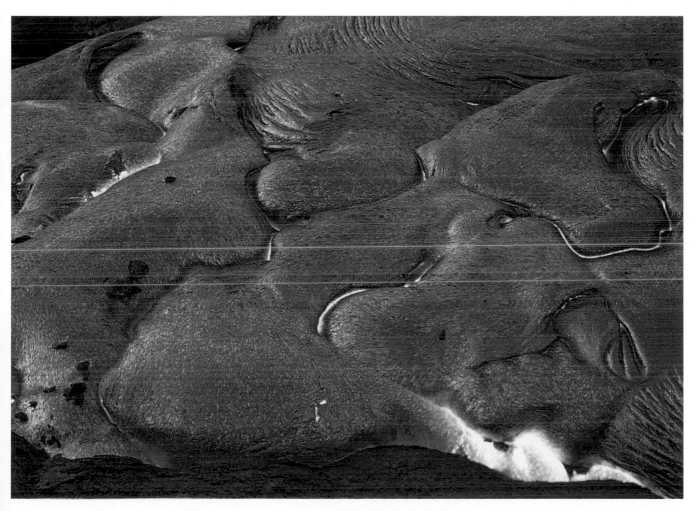

Lava "toes" form and cool on a slow-moving pāhoehoe flow.

A lava flow, fed by the high fountain in the distance, advances through the forest. Puʻu ʻŌʻō

Haleakalā, Maui.

Streams of incandescent lava illuminate the night.
Kīlauea Volcano

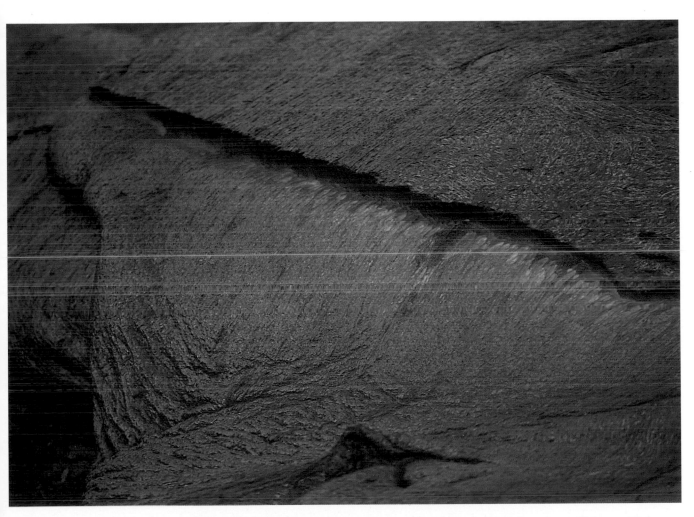

Molten lava flows beneath a layer of hardened pāhoehoe lava. Kīlauea Volcano

Fast-moving volcanic rivers let nothing obstruct their paths from the mountain to the sea.
Kīlauea Volcano

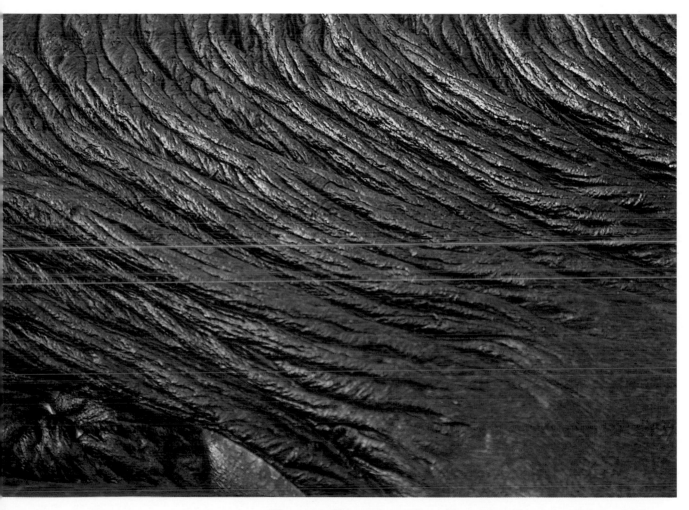

The rope-like texture of cooling pāhoehoe lava. Kīlauea Volcano

Puʻu ʻŌʻō Vent in the distance dominates the otherwise flat landscape. Kīlauea Volcano

A steaming crater of Puʻu ʻŌʻō Vent. Kīlauea Volcano

A few branches and a patch of pavement were spared by this recent lava flow.

A two-story Kalapana home flaming from an unavoidable flow.

Incandescent streams of molten rock drop from a low edge into the water beneath. Kīlauea Volcano

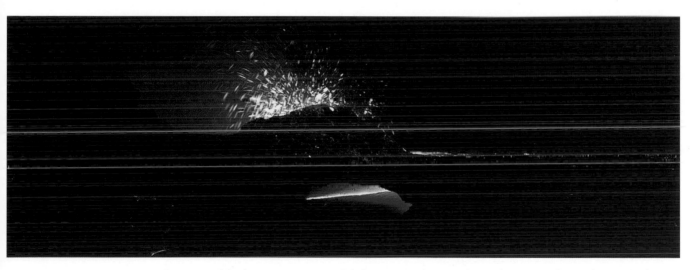

A steep-sided spatter cone with lava popping and sparking inside. Kīlauea Volcano

A dense steam marks the place where lava cools in the coastal waters. Kīlauea Volcano

Viewers admire the sunset and the steam from the lava flow. Kīlauea Volcano

Shield-shaped Mauna Loa is seen above the edge of Halemaʻumaʻu crater.

A hardened lava lake enclosed by steep crater walls. Halemaʻumaʻu Crater

These snow-filled craters were once active volcanic cones. Mauna Kea

Skiing Mauna Kea, with Mauna Loa in the background.

Mauna Loa

Haleakalā, Maui

Hualālai, with Mauna Kea in the background.